Fabian D. Falls

P.O. Box 27843

St. Louis MO 63146

All Scripture quotations, unless otherwise noted, are taken from the King James Version Bible.

Greek words and definitions are taken from Vine's Complete Expository Dictionary

English definitions taken from The American Heritage College Dictionary

First Published by Fabian D. Falls

ISBN 978-0-692-39845-6

Library of Congress Control Number: 2015904677

I thank God first for salvation and the tremendous gift to write. I thank Him for giving me a heart to care about so much and so many. I thank Him for a heart to love and obey!

I thank Him for Jesus who saved me and gave me a second chance in life!

I thank God for my wife who has been such a tremendous blessing during this journey of faith!

Fabian D. Falls

WAKE UP ZION

II CHRONICLES 7:14

FABIAN D. FALLS

If Jesus was in a situation where He was in charge of 100 sheep and one of them went astray, He would leave the 99 that were secure and in a safe place to go and get that one that was lost. Let us all have an attitude that we will step out of our normality to help someone. There are so many people in life that feel that they have no hope. There is hope for the lost and true sight for the blind. Let us all have the attitude that no matter what we go through, we will have the heart to help someone else. Let us speak to someone that we usually don't speak to, let us pray for someone we haven't seen in years. Let us forgive those that have wronged us in the past. We cannot live in our past. If we have a heart to forgive, then we can be forgiven. Let us not miss out on the true blessings of God. God is Love. Let us love one another and pray that God will heal this land, the earth and every inhabitant that lives in it.

But I say unto you, Love your enemies, bless them that curse you, do good to them that hate you, and pray for them which despitefully use you, and persecute you... Matthew 5:44

We can accomplish anything operating under the power of God's Holy Spirit. We can live a life that typically can't be lived- when God anoints us with His strength and power. I want to encourage everyone to pray that God will open our spiritual eyes and increase our spiritual muscles to fight a war that can only be won with "Love."

There is urgency for this message to be spread across the United States, and every continent, nation and land. I have a message of peace to relay to the world-a message that needs to be heard through every ear and every heart. Destruction and deceit seem to be creeping in through the crevices of our society. Hate, murder, and suicide tries to make its home and mark in the fabric of our society. In the past when we thought of war we thought of destruction and death, but I want to articulate in our hearts war through peace. I am calling all mankind to pray for peace. When I see all of the child abductions and molestations, gang activity, murders and rapes, I continue to have thoughts in my mind and heart that we will win back the streets with the power of the Holy Ghost.

Today is a new day and today things have got to change. I proclaim it and decree it in Jesus' name. If people would be honest with themselves, they would admit, along with me, that we have made some grave mistakes over the years. We have allowed some to address issues that have torn the moral fabric of our society. The devil is a liar, and today I am exposing his lies. We are not an ignorant people- We are not a pack of dogs. Satan has tried to manipulate us through the media, and every other channel he can. The books we read, the movies we watch and the programs on television, the music we listen to, and this junk that is captivating the hearts of millions on the internet. All of these different entities play a pivotal role in the shaping of our character, moral standards and our activity in our daily lives. This world has been infiltrated with hate, deceit, lies, violence, lust, and destruction. Many forms of media are driving the fact that homosexuality, sex, drugs, alcohol, and crime are some type of entertainment. All of this negativity is being pushed in many forms of marketing and advertising. In any way possible Satan and society is trying to lead people more away from God. Many groups, organizations and individuals are trying to force feed our generation a pill of destruction that we cannot accept.

My purpose in writing this book is- we as Christians are to inform every inhabitant on earth that today things must change. We cannot watch our children get murdered and abused. We can't watch our brothers and sisters being destroyed by drugs and alcohol. We can't see our loved ones being led to a pit and not do or say anything about it. So many people that are supposed to be Christians are living such carnal lives. Many people love to pray when things are going wrong in their own families, but we need to understand that someone somewhere is going through something every minute of the day.

Today I say to every person that has been washed by the blood of Jesus. Every person that confesses His precious name, I scream at the height of my capacity, "Wake Up," "Wake Up- My Brothers and Sisters Wake Up!" We used to have an enemy in our back yard, but he has come to try to sit on our front porch. Today I admonish every person that is called by the name of

Jesus Christ to throw off the facades of the past and walk in the strength and power that has been afforded to us. We have a gift and that gift is not only precious, it is powerful. Today is the awakening of the hope and love that God promised us. Today things will not be the same. If it take for you to go through your house and find every dirty magazine, every derogatory tape, every cigarette, every drug and alcohol; If it takes for you to rid yourself of weapons or whatever device that is binding your family. Do it now! Whatever Satan is using in your home to continue to bind your family, today, declare in the name of Jesus, it has got to go.

It is amazing when God gave me the title of this book. We have seen it and read it and recited it many times, but have we ever grasped the thought that this could truly change our land. I am talking about places we can't go. I am talking about people we might never see. Homelessness, joblessness and every other "ness," is cast away with everything else negative. I am talking about the "Kingdom of God." I am talking about walking in love. I am not talking about loving those you know and your own family and friends. I am talking about loving everyone. Today we love, not with lips service, but with action behind it. Whatever it takes including tough love. We must rid our homes of perversion and fear. We must do what God called us to do. And while we are doing that let us all be real. Let us be real and realize- we are warring with a real enemy, but let us be more cognizant of the fact that we serve God and through His Son, Jesus Christ, we have the victory.

Homosexuality is not right, murder and crime is not right-all this abusive behavior- fornication and adultery is not right. Because we as inhabitants on this earth have grown to a point that pleasure of inappropriate activities are so accepted, we view this as the right thing to do. Being involved in gangs, destructive behavior and "I don't care" attitudes are normal to many, but it is a lie straight from the pits of hell. Today I declare war against every disease, every addiction, every demonic activity, and every demonic force. I declare war against every witch, warlock or sorcerer. I declare in the name of Jesus that every force of Satan is destroyed and cast back to the pits of hell. I declare that people will love again, walk in peace again, walk in hope and joy again and in the name of Jesus Christ walk in righteousness. Our land can be turned around by one simple verse that is found in the Bible:

> *If my people, which are called by my name, shall humble themselves, and pray and seek my face, and turn from their wicked ways; then will I hear from heaven, and will forgive their sin, and will heal their land…..2 Chronicles 7:14*

Are we called by the name of God? Are we truly the followers of Jesus Christ?

If that is true, I want all of us to evaluate who we are and to whom we are. God describes us as His people. He states: "My People," "If My People"- I want us to really grasp that thought. The Creator of all things and all people say we are His. We are associated with the greatest force and we can be victorious. God is love and by His love this world will change. We are called by His name and we claim to Him that we serve Him, but I challenge you with this question. Is that true? If we truly served God we wouldn't have to force people to spend time with Him in prayer or to read His Word. Many people love the fact that they can claim the name of Christ, but even through this one scripture it is much more than just saying you are associated with Jesus' name.

Our land can be turned around

If we are the followers of Christ- things should change. The Holy Spirit will move in such a powerful way. The Holy Spirit will move and is moving even as I move this pen. I know that these words will be typed when you read them, but I hope you can feel the passion and the anointing of these words as I write. I know that this book will begin a revolution of love all across the land. It is time that we love. It is time that people see God for who He truly is. God is the Creator of all things and all people.

So with that in mind how can we as His followers watch as our brothers and sisters be destroyed by our enemy.

We need to humble ourselves. Too many people are filled with pride. There is too much greed and a false sense of worth put on material things. People are doing damnable things trying to chase things. They are chasing sex, pleasure and money at the expense of their own souls. Pride is ugly and deceitful. Many people die or will kill to keep a certain image. The devil is liar. Today I declare war against pride. Let it start with ourselves and let people know by your own actions that you will not be controlled by pride. Let us begin to walk in a meek spirit. Let us love like God want us to love and not walk in the deceptive clutches of pride.

It's time to pray!

It's time to pray!

Once again, it's time to pray!

Where are the people that pray and call out to God? Many people are just living lives going about their daily business and will not dedicate time to pray. We are to commune with God and get instructions from God. We can dispatch angels when we pray. I know many people that complain about things that are happening in this world, but yet fail to pray. I have a solution.

Let us begin to pray. I don't want to seem as though I am just pointing a finger. We all need to individually begin to pray more. Prayer is power released. Prayer is communing with God. Prayer is the key to get things done. God through His Son Jesus Christ is about to release the Holy Spirit in such a powerful way. Holy Spirit we pray now that you move, heal, deliver, and set free. We need a revival and a revolution and "The Time is Now!"

God also said that we must seek His face. It is time to get into a closer relationship with Christ. For the times ahead we must develop a more intimate relationship with Christ. Our hearts has to be in tune with Him. It is time to let go and let God. For so many generations we have tried to do things ourselves, but it is time to allow God to move on our behalf. When we accomplish things using our brains or either our hands, let us give God the glory instead of accrediting all things to our self. Many people with money believe in their money so much, that they will never attribute their wealth as a blessing from God.

Let us turn from our wicked ways. All of us have sinned, but this is a time that we through the power of the Holy Spirit must do away with our sin. We must stop covering up our sin and confess it and forsake it. We must repent and walk in the power we have through the Holy Spirit. We all have sinned and come short of the glory of God. Today is a different day. Today is the day that we walk in a new way.

Today is a different day for us. There are so many of us missing the mark. We are missing what God has for us. We are missing the true rewards that Heaven has afforded us. God is on the throne and He is the ruler of all that exist. I am admonishing all of my brothers and sisters to step up to the plate and hit the home run that will drive your fellow team member home. We are in this thing together. So today I make a plea. Brother and sisters wake up from the sleep that have you bound right now. I don't want to see any of you fall into the tricks and traps that Satan has planned for you. Our worship to God should be more than the view of raising our hands in service or giving a shout here and there, but our daily activity, minute by minute, and second by second should be worship unto God. I thank God that His power is working through us and we have the victory through His Son, Jesus Christ. My hopes are that people in this world will stand up and know who they are in God. I want to see God's people walking in the power and authority that God has afforded them. I want to see God's people proclaim the victory. I can't sit back anymore and watch my brothers and sisters killing one another, deceiving each other and live lives destructive to themselves and everyone around them. We need to make a difference in this world. We should make an impact, no matter how small or great. We are servants of the Most High God. I don't know what God will have me to do, but I want to do it. I want to love like He loves, walk as He walks and please only Him. I don't want to be a people pleaser, but I want God to be pleased with me. I don't like the fact that Jesus went to the cross and died a horrible death for us and so many of us seem to be playing pity pat with the devil. I want to see people lives changed and transformed. I want to see people walking away from drugs. I want to see people love again. I want what God wants. I want to see people have an intimate relationship with God. I want to see people not worried about what society thinks about their standard of morality and their love for people and God. So many people want the church world to be silent about issues that need to be addressed. Many of these issues are disgusting and immoral, but since the majority of people want the so called freedom of choice and other terms that goes with their deceit and destruction, they want people to go against God and agree with them. We should want morality and justice, but not at the sake of love. Love does not and will not harm love, but for the sake of love- we must love. I see a world that hates to live right, even when right is right. I see a world that doesn't want life to be pure and meaningful and purposeful through God. I see so much through the lenses that I have. I see a war that is being played out in our daily lives. I cannot and will not be silent about certain issues. I can't watch my family members being consumed with alcohol, I can't watch my family and friends being destroyed by drugs, I can't sit back and watch even a total stranger being consumed by destruction and not have anything to say about it. I don't care how mad Satan gets about this- I must write. I must tell the world that through Jesus Christ we have the victory. We must begin to love.

We must begin to pray. We must begin to read God's Word daily. We must begin to fast and push away our plate. I love God's people and I love all those that don't love themselves. Prayer changes things. If we could only get people to understand that by two small adjustments we can bring about a powerful change. If we could get people to read their Word every day and to pray every day, how much of a change there will be. There is power in God's Word and there is power in prayer. I will drill this home over and over again until we get it. People it is time to pray. It is time to walk in the power and authority that God has given unto us. No longer will we sit back as spectators and watch others get involved in the fight. It is our time to battle. Satan you have tricked us long enough. You have destroyed so many people and dreams in the past, but no more. It is time for the true warriors to stand up and take their positions. We can't fight a carnal fight. We must fight through the Holy Spirit and fight from our knees. It is prayer time. It is time for us to get in our Word. It is time to believe what the Word says and it is time for us to walk in victory. Lord heal on today! Lord move on today. Lord set free in Jesus name. It takes God's anointing to destroy the yoke and set the captive free. It is time for us to truly trust God. It is time for us to believe in what He says. We are soldiers in the Army of the Living God. We will not lie down and watch our fellow brothers and sisters be defeated. It is time for us to take up the hedge and stand in the gap. If you don't have a prayer life develop one today and if you don't read the Word everyday- start today. Today is going to be like no other day you had in life. Today is a day of transformation. Today is the day you put your spiritual war clothes on. Today you are going to trust God and believe Him and walk like you've never walked before. Playtime is over. It is time for us to walk in victory. We serve the Almighty God and it is time for Him to stand up in us and we show our enemy who He truly is. Prayer will change things. Prayer will change things and it is time that we make a difference in this world. Love is the key and love is the answer to all things. Love will drive a man to pray! We will love and pray our way to the victory!

40

WORDS

OF

HOPE

IF

In the event that, Supposing that or granting that, On the condition that, Although possibly, Whether

2176 hen see! surely! If, yet, but, then

God made a promise to all of us and in that promise He said if. If we as God's chosen people are willing to do our part- God is obligated to do His. If we turn to righteousness, If we seek Him God will deliver and save His people and restore the land. It comes to these two letters- "IF". He surely will move and is waiting to move on our behalf on the condition that we will turn wholly to Him. It is time out for professing and not possessing the real power of God. He will if we will!

If my people which are called by my name shall humble themselves and pray and seek my face and turn from their wicked ways then will I hear from Heaven and will forgive their sin and will heal their land

2nd Chronicles 7:14

MY

Of or belonging to me; The possessive form of I. Used as a modifier before a noun

God says that we are related to Him. And we have been given a charge to look like Him, walk like Him, and love like Him. It is a powerful thought to grasp that God will call us His. No one can take us away from Him because He says we are His. Let us understand the power we have when God says you are mine.

If my people which are called by my name shall humble themselves and pray and seek my face and turn from their wicked ways then will I hear from Heaven and will forgive their sin and will heal their land

2nd Chronicles 7:14

PEOPLE

Human beings considered as a group or in indefinite numbers. A body of persons living in the same country under one national government, a nationality, A body of persons sharing a religion, culture, language, or inherited condition of life.

6639 am people, nation, countrymen, army, troop

Collectively we have power from on High. We are a troop and a nation commissioned to bring light into a dark world. We have been commissioned to be the salt and preservative on this earth. We are a nation of love and hope. We have been chosen by God. We are an army spreading peace throughout the land. We have been gathered together for one purpose and that is to do the will of the Father. God is love and He has called us to eradicate hate through love on this earth.

If my people which are called by my name shall humble themselves and pray and seek my face and turn from their wicked ways then will I hear from Heaven and will forgive their sin and will heal their land

2nd Chronicles 7:14

WHICH

What particular one or ones in a set of things or people. The one or ones previously mentioned or implied, specifically

There is no mistake to our calling. God has called us to a specific task for this specific hour. We have to step forward and move within the dimensions that God has set forth for us. You are His chosen people and you must move now to fulfill His will for your life.

If my people which are called by my name shall humble themselves and pray and seek my face and turn from their wicked ways then will I hear from Heaven and will forgive their sin and will heal their land

2nd Chronicles 7:14

ARE

To exist, to occur, to live, to occupy a position; To have a certain identity or quality or condition- Second person singular and plural, and first and third person plural, pr. indic. of "be"

We exist for this time. We have been positioned to move in this hour. We have been given a specific role or duty to fulfill. Let us be found doing that which God has commanded us. Let us continue to seek Him for instruction and to lead us into our destiny. We are to be identified with Christ. People should know us and see a difference in us. Let us be grateful for our position in God and live a life dedicated and committed to Him.

If my people which are called by my name shall humble themselves and pray and seek my face and turn from their wicked ways then will I hear from Heaven and will forgive their sin and will heal their land

2nd Chronicles 7:14

CALLED

To say in a loud voice; announce. To demand or ask the presence of. To order to request to undertake a particular activity or work, summon. A strong inner urge or prompting. A strong impulse.

7924 qara to be called, be summoned

As the loud calling of a siren- let us hear the summons from God to assume our positions. It is time for the called out ones to take full authority and responsibility for the position to which they have been called. We are to undertake the greatest commission ever given to man. With the Love of God we are called to love people out of bondage. By our prayer to God and accepting of our calling we will walk in the victory that is provided to us. God is calling and it is time for us to answer our call.

If my people which are called by my name shall humble themselves and pray and seek my face and turn from their wicked ways then will I hear from Heaven and will forgive their sin and will heal their land

2ⁿᵈ Chronicles 7:14

BY

Close to, next to. With the help of; through. In the name of, with respect to- through the agency of or means of

God is with us and with that realization we know that we cannot fail. We have the help of God. Through His power, might and authority we have the right to move on this earth to dispel every work of darkness. God is close to us. He is with us and next to us. He is in us and works through us. Let us know who we are in God and know that we are invincible through Him

If my people which are called by my name shall humble themselves and pray and seek my face and turn from their wicked ways then will I hear from Heaven and will forgive their sin and will heal their land

2nd Chronicles 7:14

MY

Of or belonging to me; The possessive form of I. Used as a modifier before a noun

You are mine. You are a chosen vessel unto to me. Don't worry. Do not look at the situation. My thoughts are much higher than yours and my ways so much greater than your ways. You are mine. I call you "My People."

If my people which are called by my name shall humble themselves and pray and seek my face and turn from their wicked ways then will I hear from Heaven and will forgive their sin and will heal their land

2nd Chronicles 7:14

NAME

A word or words by which a person, place or thing is known or indicated; identified or an entity is designated and distinguished from others, a word or group of words used to describe or evaluate

9005 sem name, renown, fame

You are identified with me. You are already called into a great inheritance! Many of us don't understand that calling on the name of Jesus is the greatest weapon a person can ever use. The weapons of our warfare are not carnal. I am not talking about weapons that can do physical harm. I am talking about a weapon of love and peace. When we call on the name of Jesus darkness has to go. When we call on the name of Jesus disease and destruction has to go. It is all in Him and it is in the blood of the Lamb. It is in that distinguished, precious and loving name- Jesus

If my people which are called by my name shall humble themselves and pray and seek my face and turn from their wicked ways then will I hear from Heaven and will forgive their sin and will heal their land

2ⁿᵈ Chronicles 7:14

SHALL

Used before a verb in the infinitive to show, something that will take place or exist in the future. Something such as an order, a promise, a requirement, or an obligation

We shall have the victory. We shall walk in peace. We shall have everything that God has promised to us. Jesus is the way, the truth and the life. With this we know that God is obligated to take care of us and provide for us. We shall have every provision. We shall walk in love and peace. We will endure many trials, sufferings and persecutions but we are guaranteed that we will see peace. Endure your storms because peace and sunlight shall come.

If my people which are called by my name shall humble themselves and pray and seek my face and turn from their wicked ways then will I hear from Heaven and will forgive their sin and will heal their land

2nd Chronicles 7:14

HUMBLE

Having or showing a modest estimate of one's importance, not proud. Marked by meekness or modesty in behavior, attitude, or spirit, not arrogant or prideful. Showing deferential or submissive respect. Low in rank, quality, or station, unpretentious or lowly

4044 kana to be humbled, be subdued, be subjected

It is the humble and the meek spirit that can be used greatly of God. It is this nature that can use great power and not disrespect the authority of its use. The attitude of lowliness is the attribute of the God that we serve. Jesus was as a lamb led to the slaughter and opened not His mouth. He humbled himself to the will of the Father without taking an arrogant attitude about the power He displayed. Love is that way- that it will be used greatly and not take on the arrogance of prideful behavior.

If my people which are called by my name shall humble themselves and pray and seek my face and turn from their wicked ways then will I hear from Heaven and will forgive their sin and will heal their land

2ⁿᵈ Chronicles 7:14

THEMSELVES

Those ones identified with them. Used reflexively as the direct or indirect object of a verb or as the object of a preposition. Used in the same ways as himself

All of us have a powerful testimony. We can say to the world that we have an inheritance among them that are sanctified. We are blessed to be able to be counted as one of them. Only through God and the sacrificial death of His Son, can we be counted as one of those who humbled themselves. Let us not say with our mouth only, but with our words, deeds and actions- let us be truly counted among them that love the Lord.

If my people which are called by my name shall humble themselves and pray and seek my face and turn from their wicked ways then will I hear from Heaven and will forgive their sin and will heal their land

2nd Chronicles 7:14

AND

Together with; in addition to; as well as; added to; plus-and with this consequence

God has something great for us. He has planned well in advance a great celebration and victory for us. Let's work together with Him and reap all the blessings that God has promised to us. Let us reap the consequences and all the rewards of God by living a humble, loving and committed life to God.

If my people which are called by my name shall humble themselves and pray and seek my face and turn from their wicked ways then will I hear from Heaven and will forgive their sin and will heal their land

2ⁿᵈ Chronicles 7:14

PRAY

To utter a prayer or prayers, to make a fervent request or an entreaty To ask (someone) imploringly, beseech; to make a devout or an earnest request for

It is time for us to pray to God and request our needs and the needs of others. But most important it is time to pray to God and commune with Him that we will not find our will, but know the will that He has for our life. We have been given authority to speak and receive. It is time for us to walk and speak with authority. It is time for us to rebuke every negative force that comes against God and His plan for our life. It's time to pray and with our obedient walk to His commands, there is nothing that God would not grant us on Jesus' behalf. He is a prayer hearing and a prayer answering God.

If my people which are called by my name shall humble themselves and pray and seek my face and turn from their wicked ways then will I hear from Heaven and will forgive their sin and will heal their land

2nd Chronicles 7:14

AND

Together with; in addition to; as well as; added to; plus-and with this consequence

There are many things that we must do as people of God. The first thing we must do is ask God to continue to humble us. We must seek God in every area of our life, but continue to seek more and more ways that God can shape us into His image. Praying with a humble heart is great conditioning and a catalyst to a fervent heart.

If my people which are called by my name shall humble themselves and pray and seek my face and turn from their wicked ways then will I hear from Heaven and will forgive their sin and will heal their land

2nd Chronicles 7:14

SEEK

To try to locate, or discover; search for- To endeavor to obtain or reach; to go to or toward, to inquire for; request

1335 baqas to seek, search, look for, inquire about

This is a time that we should be going after God like never before. It is time for us to get close to Him and allow His Holy Spirit to burn off everything that's not like Him. It is time to discover the hidden things of God. It is time for us to reach beyond surface Christianity and live at a more intimate level with Him. It is time to go after God with our whole heart and live with integrity. Starting today let us not look at the faults of yesterday, but look at the victorious walk that we have ahead.

If my people which are called by my name shall humble themselves and pray and seek my face and turn from their wicked ways then will I hear from Heaven and will forgive their sin and will heal their land

2ⁿᵈ Chronicles 7:14

MY

The possessive form of I. Used as a modifier before a noun

I AM THAT I AM. Seek My Face! The Lord has been so good to us and as the trying times come we should remember to whom we are. The almighty God is with us and we are His. This should bring comfort to our hearts and ease our minds. The Creator of all things says that I am His so I am above every circumstance or problem that arises in my life.

If my people which are called by my name shall humble themselves and pray and seek my face and turn from their wicked ways then will I hear from Heaven and will forgive their sin and will heal their land

2nd Chronicles 7:14

FACE

A person; a person's countenance, value or standing in the eyes of others. The surface presented to view

parim The noun is sometimes used anthropomorphically of God; the Bible speaks as though He had a face. (Taken from Vine's Complete Expository Dictionary)

Yet we know that God is a spirit and He that worships Him must worship Him in Spirit and in truth.

God's face is presented to us in many ways. God's face can be found in the secret place of His tabernacle. God's face can be found in the solace place of worship. God is found in the quiet place of our heart and soul. He goes to the depth of our spirit man. God's face is found by us diligently seeking after Him with all of our heart, soul, and mind- He promises us that He will be found.

If my people which are called by my name shall humble themselves and pray and seek my face and turn from their wicked ways then will I hear from Heaven and will forgive their sin and will heal their land

2nd Chronicles 7:14

AND

Together with; in addition to; as well as; added to; plus-and with this consequence

After we have humbled ourselves, and after we begin to seek His face, we must continue to seek Him some more- we will find our Savior in the face of prayer and in the bowels of our consistency.

If my people which are called by my name shall humble themselves and pray and seek my face and turn from their wicked ways then will I hear from Heaven and will forgive their sin and will heal their land

2ⁿᵈ Chronicles 7:14

TURN

To cause to move around in order to achieve a result; to perform or accomplish by rotating or revolving; to change the direction of or course of; to change the purpose, intention, or content of by persuasion or influence. To cause to take on a specified character, nature, identity or appearance; change or transform

hapak "to turn, overturn, change, transform, turn back." "In it simplest meaning, hapak expresses the turning from one side to another, such as "turning one's back (Josh. 7:8), or as a man wipeth a dish, wiping it, and turning it upside down. (Taken from Vine's Complete Expository Dictionary)

It's time to turn from unrighteousness; it's time to turn from sin. God will expose every sin and unkind act we try to hide. Turning includes confessing, forsaking, and being cleansed from all unrighteousness. Make a turn today!

If my people which are called by my name shall humble themselves and pray and seek my face and turn from their wicked ways then will I hear from Heaven and will forgive their sin and will heal their land

2nd Chronicles 7:14

FROM

Used to indicate a specified place or time as a starting point; Used to indicate a source, a cause, an agent or instrument; Used to indicate separation, removal, or exclusion; Used to indicate differentiation

This is the place and this is the time. We must turn from our wicked ways. We must use this as the focal point for our change. I know that yesterday will not arrive tomorrow, so starting now I will move from this point to the next point of faith. I will grow from this level in my walk to an even greater dimension within my salvation. It comes from God. Jesus paid the price, so I will go from the pit to the palace.

If my people which are called by my name shall humble themselves and pray and seek my face and turn from their wicked ways then will I hear from Heaven and will forgive their sin and will heal their land

2nd *Chronicles 7:14*

THEIR

The possessive form of "they"- Used as a modifier before a noun

You, me and everyone else, we are in the same boat. We need deliverance. We need the power and strength that only comes from His Holy Spirit. We are God's chosen people and we have an inheritance to obtain. Through motivation and example let us show others the way to live, so they too may go and gain what's rightfully theirs.

If my people which are called by my name shall humble themselves and pray and seek my face and turn from their wicked ways then will I hear from Heaven and will forgive their sin and will heal their land

2nd Chronicles 7:14

WICKED

Evil by nature and in practice; playfully malicious or mischievous; severe and distressing; highly offensive; obnoxious

8273 ra evil, bad, wrong, deadly, painful, immoral, impure, vile, terrible

All have sinned and come short of the glory of God. We all have had evil ways by nature. We all have offended someone or have practiced at sin for a while to enjoy the pleasures of this world. It doesn't matter how much or how little we've done, we are all guilty of having wicked ways one way or another in our life. Sin is just what it is- disgusting and filthy. It is impure and immoral in so many ways, but thank God for the blood of Jesus and His Holy Spirit. U-turns are legal with God!

If my people which are called by my name shall humble themselves and pray and seek my face and turn from their wicked ways then will I hear from Heaven and will forgive their sin and will heal their land

2nd Chronicles 7:14

WAYS

A course that is or may be used in going from one place to another; A course of conduct or action A manner or method of doing; A usual or habitual manner or mode of being living, or acting; An individual or personal manner of behaving, acting or doing.

2006 derek way, path, route, road, journey, conduct, way of life

Our usual way of life will be interrupted today. It is lovely to know that through all the junk we've been through- there is another path for us to take. We felt ourselves that we were headed to a road of destruction and thought that we couldn't stop. It's a true blessing to know that God put the brakes on the roller-coaster that was headed downhill to destruction and death. Thank the Lord that he is the way. Without His course of action and the way that He has made we would have been doomed. Thank you Jesus for being the way!

If my people which are called by my name shall humble themselves and pray and seek my face and turn from their wicked ways then will I hear from Heaven and will forgive their sin and will heal their land

2ⁿᵈ Chronicles 7:14

THEN

At that time; next in time, space, or order; immediately afterward; as a consequence; therefore; in that case accordingly

This is our time. This is the time for salvation for all. It is time for us to stand up for our lost family and friends. It is time for us to stand in the gap for those we don't know. Strangers or enemies- it makes no difference. What's coming next is what is important. The great commission will be fulfilled, but we have to do our part.

If my people which are called by my name shall humble themselves and pray and seek my face and turn from their wicked ways then will I hear from Heaven and will forgive their sin and will heal their land

2nd Chronicles 7:14

WILL

The mental faculty by which one deliberately chooses or decides upon a course of action; volition- To choose or decide; A desire, purpose, or determination, especially of one in authority

God says that if we will, He will. I don't know about you but I can trust the fact that if God makes a promise His promise is sure. God wants us to make a decision and choose to be blessed. He wants us to choose to pray for someone else. He wants us to love our enemy and even pray for those that persecute us. God calls us to do much, but He did the most. He gave Himself for us and we should give ourselves for Him and others. Choose to love, make a decision to live a committed life to Him. If you will He will.

If my people which are called by my name shall humble themselves and pray and seek my face and turn from their wicked ways then will I hear from Heaven and will forgive their sin and will heal their land

2nd Chronicles 7:14

I

Used to refer to oneself as speaker or writer

God is the ultimate "I". He is as the scripture says, "I am the Lord that healeth thee," "I am the Lord thy God" "I AM THAT I AM." "I am the Alpha and the Omega" "I am the First and the Last"- simply put He says I am the LORD. If He says it, it shall be done. If the entire world tells me no, I will still have joy, if my hope is in the ultimate I.

If my people which are called by my name shall humble themselves and pray and seek my face and turn from their wicked ways then will I hear from Heaven and will forgive their sin and will heal their land

2*nd* Chronicles 7:14

HEAR

To perceive sound by the ear; to listen to attentively; to listen to and consider favorably

9048 sama to hear, listen, to obey, to be heard, to summon, call together, to proclaim, summon, make hear

To hear from God is an important step to deliverance and victory, but an even more endeavor is for God to hear you. We must be in a position of prayer. We must not stop the flow of fervent prayers going up to God. Allow God to hear you by petitioning Him day and night. The Lord who neither slumbers nor sleeps will hear your prayers and like a gracious Father full of love and compassion- He will answer your prayers! Put yourself in a position for God to hear you.

If my people which are called by my name shall humble themselves and pray and seek my face and turn from their wicked ways then will I hear from Heaven and will forgive their sin and will heal their land

2nd Chronicles 7:14

FROM

Used to indicate a specified place or time as a starting point; Used to indicate a source, a cause, an agent or instrument; Used to indicate separation, removal, or exclusion; Used to indicate differentiation

Hearing from God is different than hearing from the world. The world tries to persuade us into believing in the abilities of mankind, and not the creator of man. God created everything and all that is from Him is good. God has a purpose and a plan for everything. Turn from worldly thinking and begin to think like God. Seek Him, commune with Him and be able to hear from Him.

If my people which are called by my name shall humble themselves and pray and seek my face and turn from their wicked ways then will I hear from Heaven and will forgive their sin and will heal their land

2ⁿᵈ *Chronicles 7:14*

HEAVEN

The abode of God, the angels, and the souls of those who are granted salvation; an eternal state of communion with God; everlasting bliss

9028 samayim heaven (the realm of God); the heavens: place of the stars, sky, air

Jesus promised that He would go and prepare a place for us. He is in the eternal place preparing the way for us. God is awesome as He sits on His Heavenly Throne. Just the thought of Heaven brings me joy. Remember that we are passing pilgrims and Heaven is our home. Our goals and attitudes should change that we think and act like a piece of Heaven on earth. Our sights should be much higher than the temporal things that we see. It's time for us to look higher. Heaven is our goal.

If my people which are called by my name shall humble themselves and pray and seek my face and turn from their wicked ways then will I hear from Heaven and will forgive their sin and will heal their land

2ⁿᵈ Chronicles 7:14

AND

Together with; in addition to; as well as; added to; plus-and with this consequence

What a joyous time that it will be. God not only promises us blessings in the future, but He promises blessings right now. Let us begin to live like we are blessed. Let us walk like we are blessed. Let us talk like we are blessed. Let us pray and confess with our mouth blessing upon blessings. Let us pray day and night and believe what we pray. If we are fervent in prayer and walking upright before God, there is no good gift that He will withhold from us. Believe the promises of God!

If my people which are called by my name shall humble themselves and pray and seek my face and turn from their wicked ways then will I hear from Heaven and will forgive their sin and will heal their land

2ⁿᵈ Chronicles 7:14

WILL

The mental faculty by which one deliberately chooses or decides upon a course of action; volition- To choose or decide; A desire, purpose, or determination, especially of one in authority

God will heal this land. God will deliver your family and friends. God will heal and deliver. God will keep His promise to us. God is a faithful God and He requires that we be faithful to Him. God created us to commune with Him. It is time that we develop a prayer life and commune with God. Everything in life will change if we begin to walk in love and pray. Walk in love and pray. That's it. Walk in love and pray- I believe that as we begin to change our behavior about prayer- We will see a dramatic change in the course of this earth.

If my people which are called by my name shall humble themselves and pray and seek my face and turn from their wicked ways then will I hear from Heaven and will forgive their sin and will heal their land

2nd Chronicles 7:14

FORGIVE

To excuse for a fault or an offense; pardon- To renounce anger or resentment against; to absolve from payment of

6142 salach to forgive, release, pardon

Jesus went to the Cross and died for our sins. Every fault or guilt has been wiped clean by the blood of the Lamb. I love what the Bible says when it speaks about while we were yet sinners He died for us. He didn't care about our position or what we were doing. He knew we needed salvation and He provided it for us. We have been excused for every sin. He has made the payment for us. He gave His own life so that we might be forgiven. Ask God for forgiveness and forgive someone else today.

If my people which are called by my name shall humble themselves and pray and seek my face and turn from their wicked ways then will I hear from Heaven and will forgive their sin and will heal their land

2ⁿᵈ Chronicles 7:14

THEIR

The possessive form of they; Used as a modifier before a noun

Their- includes even ours today. We all need our sins forgiven. We need the power of God to show up in our lives. God spoke collectively and today we need Him to show up for us in a dramatic way. There is only one answer and one hope. The way that "they" needed Him then- we need Him now. We have been called to such a time as this. It is time for our prayers to be heard by God.

If my people which are called by my name shall humble themselves and pray and seek my face and turn from their wicked ways then will I hear from Heaven and will forgive their sin and will heal their land

2ⁿᵈ *Chronicles 7:14*

SIN

A transgression of a religious or moral law, especially when deliberate; Deliberate disobedience to the known will of God; a condition of estrangement from God

2633 hatta't sin, wrong, iniquity

The only way that our deliverance will come is that we be honest with ourselves and to be honest with God. Any man trying to deceive God does nothing but deceive himself. By our forgiveness and walking in obedience we will obtain the blessings of God. We have to begin to walk in love and obey God at all cost. There is not a little wrong, a little iniquity, and a little sin that we can get by with. Let us begin to forsake all wrong and pray with a fervent heart expecting to hear from God. If we believe that God will bring the answer He will in a mighty way.

If my people which are called by my name shall humble themselves and pray and seek my face and turn from their wicked ways then will I hear from Heaven and will forgive their sin and will heal their land

2nd Chronicles 7:14

AND

Together with; in addition to; as well as; added to; plus-and with this consequence

What a joyous time that it will be. God not only promises us blessings in the future, but He promises blessings right now. Let us begin to live like we are blessed. Let us walk like we are blessed. Let us talk like we are blessed. Let us pray and confess with our mouth blessing upon blessings. Let us pray day and night and believe what we pray. If we are fervent in prayer and walking upright before God, there is no good gift that He will withhold from us. Believe the promises of God!

If my people which are called by my name shall humble themselves and pray and seek my face and turn from their wicked ways then will I hear from Heaven and will forgive their sin and will heal their land

2nd Chronicles 7:14

WILL

The mental faculty by which one deliberately chooses or decides upon a course of action; volition- To choose or decide; A desire, purpose, or determination, especially of one in authority

This is worth repeating. God will heal this land. God will deliver your family and friends. God will heal and deliver. God will keep His promise to us. God is a faithful God and He requires that we be faithful to Him. God created us to commune with Him. It is time that we develop a prayer life and commune with God. Everything in life will change if we begin to walk in love and pray. Walk in love and pray. That's it. Walk in love and pray- I believe that as we begin to change our behavior about prayer- We will see a dramatic change in the course of this earth.

If my people which are called by my name shall humble themselves and pray and seek my face and turn from their wicked ways then will I hear from Heaven and will forgive their sin and will heal their land

2ⁿᵈ Chronicles 7:14

HEAL

To restore to health or soundness; cure- To set right, repair; to restore (a person) to spiritual wholeness

8324 rapa to heal, repair

This land is in an almost horrific state. The violence and crime that is taking place is senseless and unthinkable. There is hatred running wild in our streets. But I see a restoration taking place and all of us are a part of that restoration. God will heal His land and bring all of us to spiritual wholeness. Saints of God the battle belongs to us and the victory is ours. God will set things right and repair that which needs to be made whole. Let us live out this word that comes from Heaven and see our land healed and restored.

If my people which are called by my name shall humble themselves and pray and seek my face and turn from their wicked ways then will I hear from Heaven and will forgive their sin and will heal their land

2nd Chronicles 7:14

THEIR

The possessive form of they; Used as a modifier before a noun

When Solomon prayed this prayer to God he knew that their deliverance came only from God. He knew that by the faithful prayer of a sincere heart that God would hear and answer. Just as Solomon did it is time for us to assemble together and declare and petition God on behalf of this world. Many don't believe that things will change, but for those who believe in God and the power of prayer. It's time for us to do as Solomon did and wait on the answer from God.

If my people which are called by my name shall humble themselves and pray and seek my face and turn from their wicked ways then will I hear from Heaven and will forgive their sin and will heal their land

2ⁿᵈ Chronicles 7:14

LAND

The solid ground of the earth; A nation; a country; The people of a nation, district, or region- Territorial possessions or property; an area or realm- A tract that may be owned, together with everything growing or constructed on it.

824 eres, world, earth, land, ground, soil, country, region, territory

I am excited because now in unity the saints of God will begin to pray. Every nation, every region, every tribe and tongue will see the miraculous wonder working power of God. Let us believe God in what He says. If God instructs us to humble ourselves, to pray, seek His face and to turn from our wicked ways. If we do that He will heal this land.

If my people which are called by my name shall humble themselves and pray and seek my face and turn from their wicked ways then will I hear from Heaven and will forgive their sin and will heal their land

2nd Chronicles 7:14

People throw around the concept of prayer, but truly don't understand the natural or the supernatural authority it holds. When people pray they need to understand the seriousness and importance of the prayers they are offering to God. While we are praying we must believe that God is moving in the supernatural the moment we speak. Once we pray we must leave it in God's hand and not pray that same prayer over and over in doubt or fear. Pray the prayer and begin to thank God for doing it. When we pray in faith, we pray believing. It is time for us to take back everything that the enemy has stolen from us. I am not waiting on another homicide. I don't want another tragedy to occur for us to get serious about prayer. I don't want someone else to get hurt or killed for the community to come together and pray. I love everyone and I want to see people live victorious lives. The only way to the victory is to do as God says. Pray, humble yourself, seek His face and turn from your wicked ways. Get to the point you do as God says do. Let us be men and women of integrity. Let us be people who follow God and believes what He says. Let us move beginning today to take back the authority that God has given to us. Let us move and rebuke the enemy from stealing from us anymore. I rebuke death. I rebuke sickness. I rebuke anything that comes against the people of God. It is time that we stand up and be who God called us to be. We have the power over all the power of the enemy. We have power over all sickness and disease. We have power over every lying, cheating, demonic, adulterous, murdering, alcoholic, and drug addictive spirit. We have power over every envious, homosexual, thieving, fornicating, abusive, deceptive spirit and every demonic spirit that exist. We have power over every gossiping, cheating, and destructive spirit that comes to destroy us. We have power over every demonic force that comes against us. If we are going to be set free we have to pray our way out. If our family and friends are going to be set free, we have to pray them out. We must be in right standing with God. We as saints of God must make a decision to put down every damnable thing that hinders our walk with God. We must pray our way out and throw a hook out and pray others out, too. We must understand that we have to turn away from sin. We must forsake sin and let our prayers be heard by God. Many of us are wrapped up in the world's ways and in things that don't pertain to God at all. For many years we have set back and watched the devil destroy our families, rape and destroy our friends. We have seen so much destruction. Today we are not going to sit around any longer. How are we going to stop all the craziness that is going on in this world? That answer is found in 2nd Chronicles 7:14. God has given us the answer, but so many of us will not heed to the words and command that God has given to us. We have played games long enough. It is time for us to arise and be who God called us to be. It is not about a title or position and neither prestige. We are all on the same boat and we all need to take the ride. We need to stand in the gap and fight together. We need to stand and even kneel together in the unity of prayer. If one can put a thousand to flight and two can put ten thousand to flight- how much more can we do as Saints of God truly living and obeying God and praying in unity. We are commanded to pray, we are expected to pray, we are expected to live and walk in the authority that we have. We have all the power of Heaven at our disposal. We have power over all the works of darkness and over every demonic force that comes against us. Stand up- Saint of God and set the captives free. Use the authority that God has given to us. It is time for us to wage war and secure our victory. It is time to save those hooked on drugs. It is time for the alcoholic to be set free. It is time for people to walk in love and every bound person to be set free. It is time for murders to stop; it is time for lying, stealing, and cheating to be a thing of the past. It is time for us to wake up as Saints of God and claim the victory. It is time for us to walk in love. It is time for us to be the people God called us to be- Christians. We are to be just like Jesus when He walked this earth. He walked in divine power and we need to walk in divine power, also. We cannot have the power of Heaven behind us if we are simply playing games. We must understand the seriousness of this battle and get real -for real. I rebuke Satan on every hand, every plan, every plot, every scheme, and every demonic activity. It is time for us to pray and mean what we say. It is time for us to pray and believe what we pray. It is time for us to truly believe God and do exactly what He says. We have power over all and every enemy. Let us live with love and walk in love and do what God commissioned us to do.

Love and prayer is the key, and love and prayer is the answer. God has given us a heart to love and be compassionate about the lost. We have to get out and witness to a lost generation, a generation of people that really don't know Jesus Christ. It is up to us to give an introduction. The greatest thing we can do is live a life of love. We need to show the world Jesus Christ by the life we live. God has given us a command to turn from our wicked ways. He has told us to humble ourselves. He has told us to pray and seek His face. He understands His Words not the words of man. God is calling for a change in our life. This is a life committed to love, studying His Word, and fasting and prayer. Let us love and pray our way to the victory starting today.

After the shooting death of Michael Brown here in Ferguson Missouri sparks began to fly. After the initial anger and aftermath of the burnings and looting- I believe change is coming to this area. I not only pray for the Brown family but so many families that are losing their loved ones by senseless acts of violence around the St. Louis area. Even though I live in this area, I know that many more cities are experiencing the same devastating effects of crime, violence and sin. My prayers go out to all cities, countries and nations. I pray that God will move and come against this enemy that is plaguing our land. I pray for change because so many of our young brothers and sisters are losing their lives at a very young age. This has got to stop.

I thank God for all the beautiful souls He gave an opportunity to live on this earth. But at the same time I am upset by those beautiful ones whose life was snuffed out prematurely. On behalf of them and so many people that are going through some form of persecution, I say it is time for us to react.

I attended the Ferguson Unity event in February 2015, and I was able to hear from (Billy Graham's grandson) Will Graham, Pastor Tony Shaw of Ferguson Baptist Church, Aeneas Williams- Pastor and former NFL player, and Dr. Tony Evans, Pastor of Oak Cliff Fellowship in Dallas TX. This was a powerful event and I was so grateful to be in the same room with these great men of God. I am taking the message of every one of these men and becoming more active in my community. I am making a pledge to seek God with openness and honesty. I pray that my life will be one of commitment and integrity. I pray that someone will see the true transformation that has taken place in my life and want the same change for theirs. If I were to give a summation of the event I would say that it was a call to be real. It was a call for us to repent of our sins and run away from them so that we can be heard by God. I believe that God is going to move so powerfully in this area and that a revival will spring forth as people become serious about God again. It may be a way to vent but I thank God for giving me the vision to write this book. I thank Him for giving me a desire to see change for our community. It is time for us to pray, but as we pray we have to be real in our endeavors. We should not be praying for the sake of praying, knowing that our prayers are not being heard nor answered by God. It is time out for the formality- having church on Sundays and bible studies on mid-week is not the solution to our problems. Our solution is found in God. Our solution is found in us praying to God with sincere and pure hearts. I am making it plain as I know how. There are so many people out here going through the motions and dressed impressively nice. But all the outer appearance of holiness and righteousness is showing up on the streets and in the homes of our families. We can see it in the media, main stream news and in the venues we call entertainment and art. We can see it in our government and our educational system. It is corrupting our schools, laws, and even our health and social value systems. Lord, help us and please forgive us. Please allow us another chance to get it right. We are looking for a heavenly home and we understand that we are passing pilgrims, but while we are here Lord please allow us to affect this land. Please Lord; bring more souls into your Kingdom. Allow the slacking and slothful to become serious and sold-out. Please help every leader to overcome the bondage and sin that is truly blocking their blessings. Allow your Holy Spirit to move freely in your churches and in your land that people might live and have Godly homes. Help every level of society. Help us all Lord. Let us change and speak the truth to one another and not cover each other's sins. Let us expose one another in love that your plan may go forth in this earth. Let us love and not tolerate the sin and junk that is going on right now. Let us all change. Start with me first Lord. Heavenly Father, forgive me for any and all wrong and sin. Forgive me for anything knowingly or unknowingly. I confess and repent of any and all sin. I want to be real and I want to be right. Expose me if I try to sneak, creep or do anything against your will. I want to live for you and I want your purpose to be lived in and through me. Help me through your Holy Spirit. Thank you for saving me through your Son. Thank you for a second chance. Thank you for sending revival, thank you for healing this land for your Kingdom. Thank you moving in your power and touching the hearts of men and women, boys and girls that will give their life to you. I thank you for it all in Jesus' name. Amen.

I will be the first to tell you that I don't know all the ways of God. I can't tell you how and when the end will come. What I do know is that we can claim the promises of God. While the battle wages on, that doesn't mean that we should sit by indolent not doing anything about the turmoil that is affecting our land. Let us fight the true fight of faith. Let us live and pray like we've never prayed before. Let us pray with conviction and let us pray with power. Let us pray knowing that something is going to happen. Let us believe God and pray His Word back to Him. And when we pray in faith we know we will get the results we're expecting. Thank the Lord for His Word and I thank Him for His will. I believe God is about to do a very powerful thing with the sold-out believers that still believe in His supernatural power. God help us and help your people. There are so many people out there who need to know about Jesus. God there are so many people that need to feel and know your love. How dare we continue to use your name and not be who you say we are! How dare me not to live the way you created me to live. Some may say that this is Old Testament and we should not be using this scripture for this context, but for this context we had better use it to bring glory to His name. We won't have a context if we don't use this context to bring God's glory as the true manifestation and the only context. God's Holy Spirit needs to be present and moving in our churches. God's Holy Spirit needs to be moving and directing our lives. It is time out for this phony, pretentious stuff we are experiencing right now. God send your Holy Spirit to wake us up and change us now. We need you Lord. Let us pray. Let us be real. Please help us and wake us up. Wake up Zion, please Wake up, now!

WHEN I KNEEL THINGS BEGIN TO HEAL

As I hear babies crying and see mothers dying

As I see violence increase and Satan keeps lying

As I see brothers killing brothers

And see so many people hating one another

As I see child molestation and teen pregnancy

As I see alcoholism, drug addiction and homosexuality

As I see the world seem to be overcome with hate

I will continue to live for the Lord and always pray

As I see mental disorders and suicide

And see people living with no hope inside

As I see people being affected with AID's and poverty

And people dying from cancer, heart disease and diabetes

As I see people dying from all types of disease

I will continue to stay on my knees

Regardless of what's going on

And how it makes me feel

I know, *"When I kneel things begin to heal"*

Fabian D. Falls

Fabian D. Falls